# UNSOLVED
## HISTORICAL
# MYSTERIES

by Allison Lassieur

Raintree is an imprint of Capstone Global Library Limited, a company incorporated in England and Wales having its registered office at 7 Pilgrim Street, London, EC4V 6LB – Registered company number: 6695582

**www.raintree.co.uk**
myorders@raintree.co.uk

Edited by Aaron Sautter
Designed by Sarah Bennett
Picture research by Gina Kammer
Production by Morgan Walters
Printed in China

ISBN 978 1 4747 0580 6
19 18 17 16 15
10 9 8 7 6 5 4 3 2 1

**British Library Cataloguing in Publication Data**
A full catalogue record for this book is available from the British Library.

**Acknowledgements**
Alamy: © John Morrison, 21, © Mary Evans Picture Library, 7, © Robert Estall photo agency, 18; Corbis: National Geographic Creative/© Keenpress, 23; Getty Images: De Agostini Picture Library, 11, Sovfoto, 23; Granger, NYC: 27; Shutterstock: American Spirit, 29, Antlio, (background) 16-17, 19, Claire McAdams, (fog smoky background) throughout, djgis, 10-11, Janece Flippo, 15, Jon Bilous, (background) 12-13, Mark Heider, (Earth map) throughout, Milosz_G, (background) 22-23, 24-25, MisterElements, (ink splatters) throughout, Roobcio, (grunge background) throughout, seahorsetwo, 4, Steve Heap, (background) 18, TAGSTOCK1, cover, 16-17, Ursa Major, (worn background) throughout; Wikimedia: 13, 14, (inset) 21, Beinecke Rare Book & Manuscript Library, Yale University, 6-7, 8, 9

We would like to thank Tim Solie, Adjunct Professor of History, for his invaluable help in the preparation of this book.

Every effort has been made to contact copyright holders of material reproduced in this book. Any omissions will be rectified in subsequent printings if notice is given to the publisher.

All the internet addresses (URLs) given in this book were valid at the time of going to press. However, due to the dynamic nature of the internet, some addresses may have changed, or sites may have changed or ceased to exist since publication. While the author and publisher regret any inconvenience this may cause readers, no responsibility for any such changes can be accepted by either the author or the publisher.

# Contents

# Mysteries that time can't solve

Secret codes that no one can solve. People who disappear forever. Treasures that vanish without a trace. These historical mysteries, and others, have stumped people for hundreds or even thousands of years.

How can these mysteries go unsolved for so long? Sometimes facts get lost or forgotten. Records are often destroyed. People who may know things die. And sometimes no one cares about the mystery when it happens. It is only later that someone wonders what happened, and then tries to solve the mystery.

But all mysteries have clues somewhere. Clues may be hidden in a forgotten book. Perhaps the answers lie in the faded memories of someone who saw something happen long ago. Old codes can be broken, missing people can be found and lost treasures can be dug up. Let's take a look at some of history's most baffling mysteries.

# The book that can't be read

One of the world's biggest unsolved mysteries is hidden among the rare books in the library of Yale University in the United States. Most people don't even know it's there. Those who do know about it don't know how to read it. It's known as the Voynich **manuscript**, and is a strange old book that no one has ever been able to read or understand.

Almost nothing is known about the book's origins. It was written more than 500 years ago in the 1400s, and it was probably made in Italy. But nobody knows who wrote it or why.

This mysterious book looks similar to other **medieval** books of the time period. It's written with beautiful looping handwriting, and is full of drawings of plants and the night sky. But take a closer look and things start to get strange. The drawings of plants are of no known plants on Earth. The text is also written in a strange unknown language.

Wilfrid Voynich researched and collected many rare books across Europe during the early 1900s.

Rare book collector Wilfrid Voynich discovered this strange book in 1912. He found it while looking through a collection of other old books at a castle in Italy. Voynich tried to crack the manuscript's code, but failed. For nearly 100 years, expert **cryptographers** have tried to unlock the book's secrets. But nobody has been able to work it out.

**manuscript** document, such as a book or an article

**medieval** having to do with the period of European history between AD 500 and 1450

**cryptographer** person who makes and breaks codes

**7**

## What's it about?

If someone were to crack the manuscript's code, what would they learn? Experts have guessed that the book might be a scientific work written in a forgotten language. Some people think the book is full of secret knowledge written in an unknown ancient code. But others feel the Voynich manuscript is just an impressive fake. They think someone created it to fool the world into thinking he or she was an experienced doctor. But until the book's secrets can be revealed, no one will know the truth.

# Clues to cracking the Voynich code

Professor Stephen Bax is a language professor at the University of Bedfordshire, UK. As with everyone else, the Voynich manuscript perplexed him until he had an idea. He began looking for proper names listed next to the manuscript's strange pictures. He then compared the names to other old manuscripts and ancient languages. Bax soon began recognizing some words. He managed to decode the name Taurus next to a group of star drawings. He also identified several plant names scattered through the text. Bax hopes to one day translate the whole manuscript and solve the mystery for good.

The Voynich manuscript's drawings of strange plants, diagrams and star charts have baffled researchers for many years.

# The ship that went nowhere

Most ghost ships are not the spooky kind said to be haunted by ghosts or spirits. Instead, most ghost ships are vessels that have been deserted. Crew members and passengers seem to simply vanish without a trace. On 4 December 1872, Captain David Moorehouse found one of these ghost ships. He was sailing between the Azores islands and Portugal when his crew spotted a ship drifting on the waves. They had found the *Mary Celeste*, which had sailed from New York, USA, eight days before.

But something was wrong. Nobody was on the ship. When the boat set sail, on board were Captain Briggs, his wife and child, and seven crewmen. Captain Moorehouse knew the *Mary Celeste* was supposed to be in Italy. He ordered his crew to investigate the ship. They found it to be in good shape. The crew's belongings were still in place. The cargo was still intact. And there was plenty of food and water. Despite this, the ship's lifeboat and **navigation** equipment were missing. It was clear that everyone had abandoned ship. But what made them leave behind a seaworthy ship full of supplies?

Some people thought pirates might have attacked the *Mary Celeste* and captured the ship's crew. Others suggested that the crew **mutinied** and forced everyone to leave the ship. Either way, none of the ship's crew or passengers were ever seen again. No one has ever discovered the answer to what happened on the *Mary Celeste*.

**navigation** using instruments and charts to find your way in a ship or other vehicle

**mutiny** to revolt against the captain of a ship

# The mysterious treasure map

Somewhere under the green hills of Virginia, USA, a huge treasure is rumoured to lie hidden. Only one clue about the treasure exists: a written message in three parts. But this message was written in a secret code that no one has ever completely broken.

The mysterious story began in 1885 with a **pamphlet** that told the remarkable story of Thomas Beale. He had supposedly made a fortune mining gold and silver in the Wild West in the 1820s. According to the story, Beale later buried his huge treasure in Bedford County, Virginia. To keep its location safe he created three messages in coded **ciphers**. One message is thought to explain where the treasure is hidden. The second supposedly describes how much treasure there is. The third is believed to be a list of Beale's fellow miners and their families. Beale locked the messages in an iron box, which he gave to his trusted friend, Robert Morriss, for safekeeping.

According to the story, Morriss later got a letter from Beale explaining the mysterious ciphers. The letter told Morriss to wait 10 years before opening the box. In the meantime, Beale planned to send another letter with the key to the codes.

The Beale ciphers were made up of a series of seemingly random numbers.

71, 194, 38, 1701, 89, 76, 11, 83, 1629, 48, 94, 63, 132, 16,
111, 95, 84, 341, 975,14, 40, 64, 27, 81, 139, 213, 63, 90, 1120,
18, 40, 74, 758, 485,604, 230, 436, 664, 582,
124, 211, 486, 225, 401, 370,11, 101,
98, 193, 145, 1, 94, 73, 416, 918,
36, 219, 27, 176, 130, 10, 460, 25,
3,118, 320, 138, 36, 416, 280, 15,
88, 61, 304, 12, 21,24, 283, 134,
184, 360, 780, 18, 64, 463, 474,
4, 581, 34, 69, 128, 367, 460, 17,
03, 862, 70, 60, 1317, 471, 540,
568,614, 13       19, 812,

**pamphlet** small booklet

**cipher** code that uses numbers or symbols to represent letters of the alphabet

**13**

## The mystery grows deeper

Unfortunately for Morriss, the second letter with the key never came. Beale had apparently disappeared. Nobody knew what happened to him, and Morriss never heard from him again.

Despite this, Morriss kept his promise. He didn't open the box until 1845. But it made no difference. He spent years trying to decode the messages. After Morriss died the papers eventually fell into the hands of James Ward. Ward claimed to solve the second cipher, but couldn't work out the others. Eventually he grew tired of the mystery and published the pamphlet. Treasure hunters have been trying to crack the code and find the treasure ever since.

Some people say the pamphlet was a **hoax** and that the ciphers can't be solved. They say that Thomas Beale wasn't even a real person, and that Ward made up the whole story. It's possible that the whole thing is a fake. With few solid clues, it seems no one will ever know the truth.

THE

# BEALE PAPERS,

CONTAINING

AUTHENTIC STATEMENTS

REGARDING THE

# TREASURE BURIED

IN

1819 AND 1821,

NEAR

BUFORDS, IN BEDFORD COUNTY, VIRGINIA.

AND

WHICH HAS NEVER BEEN RECOVERED.

PRICE FIFTY CENTS.

LYNCHBURG:
VIRGINIAN BOOK AND JOB PRINT.
1885.

**hoax** trick to make people believe something that is not true

# Breaking the second Beale cipher

It sounds like something out of a Hollywood film. The second Beale cipher was cracked using the US Declaration of Independence. Ward claimed that he numbered each word in the Declaration. Then he matched the numbers with the coded message. The first letter of each code word spelt out the secret message. It said the treasure was buried "about four miles from Buford's" in an underground vault.

It's thought that if the vault is real, it may be full of thousands of kilograms of gold, silver and jewels.

# The Green Children of Woolpit

In the mid-1100s wolves commonly roamed the dark and dangerous forests around Woolpit in England. Villagers often dug deep pits to trap the beasts, which is how the village got its name.

But one afternoon, men working in the fields got a shock. They found two young children, a girl and a boy, in one of the wolf pits. The children's skin was a bright green colour. They wore clothing made of materials that no one recognized. And they spoke a language no one could understand.

The farmers took the children to a local landowner, Sir Richard de Calne. He kindly offered them food and water, but the children burst into tears. They refused to eat anything other than raw green beans. The green children ate nothing but the beans for months until they became used to other food.

Slowly the green colour faded from the children's skin. They also learnt to speak some English and began telling people a fantastic story. They said they were a brother and sister from a strange place called St Martin's Land. The sun never shined there. The light was always like twilight, and everything was green – even the people.

A banner in St Mary's Church in Woolpit shows the story of the Green Children and the last sighting of wild wolves in England.

## Where did they come from?

The mysterious children said they had been herding their father's animals when they wandered into a cave. Inside the cave they heard bells. They followed the sound until they were blinded by bright sunlight. When they came out of the cave, the children found themselves stuck in the wolf pit.

Could this strange story be true? Did two green children just mysteriously appear out of nowhere? Many people think this tale is just a fantastic legend. However, there is evidence that the children were real. At the time, two men researched the mystery and wrote down the stories people told about the green children. One of them even spoke to Sir Richard de Calne about his personal experience with the children.

If the green children were real, where did they come from? One idea states that they were **refugees** from another country who spoke a different language. But what could have caused the children's skin to be green? Some people think they may have been suffering from **malnutrition** or **arsenic** poisoning, which can turn the skin green. The truth about the green children is a mystery that may never be solved.

**refugee** person forced to flee his or her home because of natural disaster or war

**malnutrition** condition caused by a lack of healthy foods in a person's diet

**arsenic** poisonous chemical

**19**

# The Holy Grail of mysteries

Shugborough Hall, a grand mansion in Staffordshire, UK, holds many secrets. But its biggest secret is not inside its 300-year-old walls. Hidden among the surrounding gardens stands a weather-worn stone monument. Look closely and you'll see a mysterious series of letters carved into the stone. Some people think the letters may be a clue to one of the biggest mysteries in the world – the lost **Holy Grail**.

The letters aren't the only part of the mystery. The image above the letters has secrets of its own. It is based on a painting by Nicolas Poussin, who was rumoured to be a **Templar**. Members of the Templars were said to be the eternal guardians of the Holy Grail. Poussin is thought to have hidden clues about the Grail in his painting. Some people believe the coded letters and hidden clues are connected. They think that if this mystery was solved, the location of the Holy Grail would be discovered.

**Holy Grail** legendary cup or bowl that was believed to be used by Jesus Christ at the Last Supper

**Templar** knight of a secret religious military order during the early 1100s

No one knows if the stories about the stone inscription and the Grail are true. Some people think the carved letters are actually a coded love letter. Others think they may be a coded verse from the Bible. Many have tried to crack the code, but all have failed. Even famous code breakers during World War II (1939–1945) couldn't work it out. Today, the mystery still lingers, waiting to be solved.

O·U·O·S·V·A·V·V

D·                    M·

# The mystery of the missing amber

It was once called "The Eighth Wonder of the World". Its extraordinary beauty stunned visitors to Catherine Palace in St Petersburg, Russia. This incredible treasure was called The **Amber** Room. It was covered with more than 5 tonnes of rich amber panels and semi-precious stones. People marvelled at how the room "glowed a fiery gold" when all 565 candles were lit.

The Amber Room was the treasure of kings. It was first given to Russia's Peter the Great as a gift from the King of Prussia in 1716. It stayed in St Petersburg until 1755 and was then moved to Catherine Palace. The room's fate changed, however, when World War II broke out and Germany invaded Russia.

**amber** yellow-brown substance formed from fossilized tree resin; amber is often used in jewellery and other works of art

Taken in 1917, this is the only existing colour photograph of the Amber Room before World War II.

By then, Catherine Palace had become a museum. Its caretakers knew the Germans usually stole any art and treasure they could find. They frantically tried to move the amber panels to safety. Unfortunately, the panels were old and brittle and couldn't be moved easily. So the caretakers covered up the rich amber with wallpaper instead. But this didn't fool the German soldiers. They found the room, packed the precious panels into crates and sent them to Konigsberg, Germany.

## An unknown fate

For a time the Amber Room was installed at the Konigsberg castle museum. But the castle was bombed in 1944 – destroying the treasured room in a fiery blaze.

But was it truly destroyed? In the chaos and destruction of war, it's possible the Amber Room survived after all. For the last 70 years treasure hunters and historians have tried to discover what really happened. Some witnesses swear the room was destroyed, but others claimed to see heavy crates at the railway station near the castle. It's possible that the crates held the amber panels and were buried in secret bunkers outside the city. Some people also thought the panels were loaded onto a ship, which then sank in the Baltic Sea.

In 1997, German police found one of the jewelled amber panels. Its owner had received it from his soldier father. He claimed he didn't know where the panel had come from, but the find encouraged treasure hunters to keep searching. Since then, many have claimed to find the Amber Room. But all the reports have been false so far. The treasured room remains missing to this day.

A replica of the Amber Room was opened in Catherine Palace in St Petersburg, Russia, in 2003.

# The mysterious lost colony

History is full of cases of missing people. These people are often found alive and well, but sometimes they are never discovered. Four hundred years ago, an entire **colony** of people disappeared – and their fate remains a mystery to this day.

In 1587, John White arrived in North America with 117 English men, women and children. They hoped to build a settlement on Roanoke Island, just off the coast of present-day North Carolina. It was the second time British colonists had tried to settle at Roanoke. Another small group had tried before, and failed. But White's group had more people and supplies. Surely they would survive.

Later that year, White returned to England to gather more supplies for the new settlement. While he was there, war broke out between England and Spain. It was then too dangerous for ships to leave England. White was forced to stay until 1590.

**colony** place that is settled by people from another country and is controlled by that country

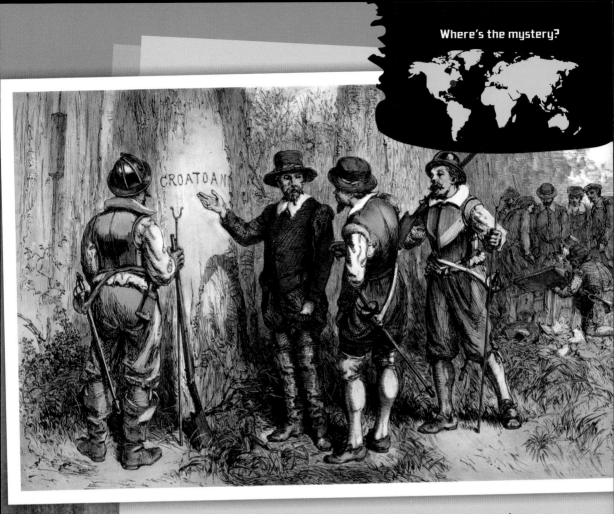

The only solid clue to the fate of the Roanoke colony was the word "Croatoan" carved into a large fence post.

When he finally returned, the ship's crew blew trumpets to let the settlers know they had arrived. But nobody answered. It was strangely quiet. The houses had been taken down and the area was deserted. There were no bodies or other signs of attack. Where had everyone gone? There were only two clues: the word "Croatoan" carved into a wooden fence post, and the letters "Cro" carved into a tree.

**27**

## All are lost

White wasn't very worried at first. Before he had left the colony, the settlers had agreed on a plan if something happened. They would get help from the Croatoans, an American Indian tribe near the Roanoke settlement.

White planned to search for the missing settlers among the Croatoan Indians. But before he could begin, a fierce storm hit the coast. White and his crew were forced to sail back to England. White died soon after he returned to England, never knowing what happened at Roanoke. A few search parties did return to look for the colonists, but the missing people were never found.

Where did the people go? Perhaps they joined the Croatoan people or one of the other tribes in the area. Perhaps they were all kidnapped and killed. It could be that they died of disease – but no bodies were ever found. One theory says the colonists moved and rebuilt the settlement in another place. The fate of the Roanoke colony remains one of the most mysterious unsolved mysteries in history.

Whether it's missing people, strangely coded documents or lost treasures, many people are fascinated by history's puzzling mysteries. It's possible that these mysteries will never be solved. But historians will keep hunting for the clues that lead them to the answers.

# Glossary

**amber**  yellow-brown substance formed from fossilized tree resin; amber is often used to make jewellery and other works of art

**arsenic**  poisonous chemical

**cipher**  code that uses numbers or symbols to represent letters of the alphabet

**colony**  place that is settled by people from another country and is controlled by that country

**cryptographer**  person who makes and breaks codes

**hoax**  trick to make people believe something that is not true

**Holy Grail**  legendary cup or bowl that was believed to be used by Jesus Christ at the Last Supper

**malnutrition**  condition caused by a lack of healthy foods in a person's diet

**manuscript**  handwritten document, such as a book or article

**medieval**  having to do with the period of European history between AD 500 and 1450

**mutiny**  revolt against the captain of a ship

**navigation**  using instruments and charts to find your way in a ship or other vehicle

**pamphlet**  small booklet

**refugee**  person forced to flee his or her home because of natural disaster or war

**Templar**  knight of a religious military order during the early 1100s

# Books

*Ancient Treasures* (Treasure Hunters), Nick Hunter (Raintree, 2013)

*The Bermuda Triangle* (Solving Mysteries with Science), Jane Bingham (Raintree, 2013)

*Sea Mysteries* (Legends of the Sea), Sian Smith (Raintree, 2011)

# Websites

**www.bbc.co.uk/history/forkids**
Discover more about world history! Uncover the answers about many famous historical mysteries.

**www.bbc.co.uk/history/british/hg_gallery.shtml**
Learn more about the story of the Holy Grail and the mystery surrounding this legendary artefact.

**www.bbc.co.uk/history/code_breaking**
Find out more about code breakers through history, as they race to uncover secrets and solve mysteries!

# Index